Ken's Story Part 1

I Talk You Talk Press

Copyright © 2018 I Talk You Talk Press

ISBN: 978-4-909733-07-8

www.italkyoutalk.com

info@italkyoutalk.com

CONTENTS

I Talk You Talk Press

INTRODUCTION

Ken Maeda is from Chiba. He is thirty-four.

Yumiko Saito is from Tokyo. She is thirty-five.

Saho Mochida is from Yokohama. She is thirty-one.

Ken, Yumiko and Saho work for a large company in Tokyo. They are all very good friends with each other. They have been friends for many years. They enjoy working together, and they enjoy going to restaurants together.

Important!

This story is set in Japan. In the story, there are some Japanese words.

The Japanese words are:

1. *o-miai* - an introductory meeting / a formal marriage interview
2. *san* - Mr/Ms (E.g. Tanaka san = Mr Tanaka)
3. *chan* - the diminutive form of san. Used for friends, family or children (E.g. Kitty chan, Jane chan)
4. *konkatsu* - searching for a marriage partner
5. *kacho* - section manager
6. *bucho* - department manager

CHAPTER ONE

Ken is a businessman. He works for a large company in Shinjuku, Tokyo. He is a very hard worker and a very nice man. His co-workers and his boss like him very much. He joined the company ten years ago. In his section there are five workers and the section manager. Everyone is very friendly and kind. His co-workers, Yumiko and Saho, are his best friends. They talk about many things. He likes Yumiko and Saho very much.

Ken works from Monday to Friday. Every day, he goes to work by train. He arrives at the office at 8:15am. He works until 7:00pm. After work, he often goes to the gym. Sometimes, he goes drinking with his co-workers. Ken enjoys his life, but there is one problem. He wants to get married, but he cannot find a marriage partner. Last year, he had three dates. He liked the women, but the women all said "No thank you!" He was very disappointed. Then, he went to two big singles parties. He talked to many women. He gave one woman his email address, but she didn't email him.

Last weekend, Ken had a date. The woman was his friend's friend. They went to a restaurant. He had a good time. After the date, he emailed the woman.

He wrote:

---*Thank you very much. I had a good time. Would you like to go for dinner next week?*---

She answered:

---*Sorry. I am busy next week.*---

He wrote:
---*Okay. Would you like to go for dinner next month?*---
She answered:
---*Sorry. I am busy next month.*---
Ken gave up.
Ken really wants to get married. But, why don't women want to see him again?

It is Monday morning. Ken walks into the office.
"Good morning!" says Ken.
"Good morning Ken," says Yumiko. "How are you?"
"I'm not so good today Yumiko," says Ken.
"Really? What's wrong?" asks Yumiko.
"I had a date on Saturday," says Ken.
"That's great! Did you have a good time?" asks Yumiko.
"Yes, I had a good time," says Ken.
"Are you going to see the woman again?" asks Yumiko.
"No, I'm not," says Ken.
"Why not?" asks Yumiko.
"I emailed the woman yesterday, but she answered 'I'm busy!'" says Ken.
"Oh, that's too bad," says Yumiko. She looks at Ken's face. He looks so disappointed. She is worried about him.
Saho walks into the office.
"Good morning!" says Saho with a big smile.
"Good morning Saho!" say Ken and Yumiko.
"Ken, are you okay? You look sad," says Saho.
"Ken is not okay," says Yumiko.
"Why not? What's wrong?" asks Saho,
"He had a date on Saturday, but the woman doesn't want to see him again," says Yumiko.
"Why doesn't she want to see you again Ken?" asks Saho.
"I don't know," says Ken. "I have many dates, and I go to singles parties. But, the women don't want to see me again! I don't know why!"
"It's strange," says Yumiko. "Ken, you are a very nice man. You are very friendly and kind. I don't understand."
"Yes, it's strange," says Saho.
"But I have another date on Saturday," says Ken. "The woman is

from an Internet dating site."

"Really? That's good!" says Yumiko.

"Yes, but I'm very nervous and very worried," says Ken. "Women always say 'No!' when I ask to see them again."

Yumiko thinks about Ken's problem. Then, she says, "Ken, I have a good idea! We can help you!"

"Help me? How?" asks Ken.

"Where are you going to meet the woman?" asks Yumiko.

"I'm going to meet her at the Italian restaurant, Casa," says Ken.

"Saho, are you busy on Saturday night?" asks Yumiko.

"No, I don't have any plans," says Saho.

"Saho, let's go to the Italian restaurant on Saturday night!" says Yumiko.

"Why?" asks Saho.

"In the restaurant we can watch Ken. We can check his manners. Then, we can give him advice. He is very nice, but women always say 'no'. That's very strange. He needs help and advice," says Yumiko.

"That's a great idea!" says Saho. "Yes, let's do that! We are like spies! We will spy on you Ken!"

"Now I feel very nervous!" says Ken. Everyone laughs.

CHAPTER TWO

It is 6:50pm on Saturday evening. Ken is sitting in the restaurant. He is waiting for the woman. Yumiko and Saho are sitting at the next table. Ken is very nervous.

Yumiko looks at Ken and says, "Ken! Relax!"

"I'm trying to relax!" says Ken.

The woman walks into the restaurant. She is very cute. Ken stands up.

"Good evening. I'm Ken Maeda. Nice to meet you," says Ken.

"Good evening. I'm Asuka Nagai. Nice to meet you too," says the woman.

They sit down. The waiter brings the menu. Ken and Asuka look at the menu.

There are many nice dishes on the menu. Ken likes Italian food very much. He looks at the menu for five minutes.

The waiter comes back. "What would you like?" the waiter asks.

"Meat sauce pasta, please" says Asuka.

"What would you like?" the waiter asks Ken.

Ken looks at the menu.

"I don't know. Hmmm…the meat sauce pasta looks good….but I had pasta for dinner last night…so…maybe pizza…" says Ken.

"Pizza? Which pizza would you like?" asks the waiter.

"Hmm…the cheese pizza looks delicious and the seafood pizza looks good, too. I don't know…" says Ken.

"The cheese pizza is today's special," says the waiter.

"Really? OK, I'll have the cheese pizza, please," says Ken.

5

"What would you like to drink?" asks the waiter.

"Let's have a bottle of wine," says Ken. "Would you like red, or white?"

"I don't drink alcohol," says Asuka. "I'll have an iced-tea, please."

"Oh really? You don't drink alcohol? Wow! OK, I will have a glass of red wine, please," says Ken.

Ken is very nervous. When he is nervous, he talks a lot. He talks about his job, his family and his hobbies. Asuka listens to his stories.

The waiter brings the food and drink. Asuka eats her pasta and Ken eats his pizza. The pizza is very delicious. Ken eats it very quickly.

Asuka finishes her pasta. The waiter comes back.

"Would you like a dessert?" asks the waiter.

"Yes, please!" says Ken. "What desserts do you have?"

"We have chocolate cake, cheesecake and strawberry cake, ice-cream and..."

"Oh, I will have the chocolate cake!" says Ken. "I love chocolate cake!"

"I will have the strawberry cake," says Asuka.

They eat the desserts. Asuka goes to the toilet. Ken looks at Yumiko and Saho. Yumiko and Saho look very angry!

Ken doesn't understand. *Why are they angry?*

CHAPTER THREE

It is Monday morning.

Ken, Yumiko and Saho are in the office. They are talking about Ken's date.

"Did I pass?" asks Ken.

"No…you didn't. You failed," says Yumiko, shaking her head. "Ken, your manners were not good in the restaurant."

"I was very shocked," says Saho.

"Why? What did I do?" asks Ken. He doesn't understand.

"First, you didn't ask Asuka 'what would you like?'" says Saho.

"Is that bad?" asks Ken.

"Yes! Of course it's bad!" says Saho.

"Why?" asks Ken.

"If you ask 'what would you like?' Asuka will think you are very kind. She will think 'He is thinking about me! He cares about me!' But you didn't think about Asuka. You only thought about yourself!" says Saho.

"Oh, I see," says Ken. "Ladies first?"

"Yes!" says Saho. "Of course!"

"Then, you looked at the menu for five minutes!" says Yumiko.

"Is that bad?" asks Ken.

"Of course! You should decide quickly!" says Yumiko. "Women like strong men who decide quickly!"

"Then, you said, 'Let's have a bottle of wine'. You should say 'What would you like to drink?'" says Saho. "Asuka said 'I don't drink alcohol'. Then, you said 'Wow!' That is not polite!"

7

"And you talked a lot! You talked about yourself! You didn't ask any questions! You didn't ask Asuka about her job, or her life," says Yumiko.

Ken looks upset. "I was nervous! I always talk a lot when I'm nervous," he says.

"I understand. But, you have to ask some questions too!" says Yumiko.

"Then, the waiter asked, 'Would you like a dessert?' You said, 'Yes, please'. You should ask the woman, 'Would you like a dessert?'"

Ken feels very bad. "I'm not good at dating," says Ken. "I'm not a good man."

"No! No! You are a very good man, Ken!" says Yumiko. "We like you very much! You are a very good friend! But you need to study dating manners!"

"Yes. You are a good man. But on dates, you get nervous. You need to relax," says Saho. "When is your next date?"

"I have an o-miai introduction meeting next month. The woman is my mother's friend's daughter," says Ken.

"Where is the meeting?" asks Saho.

"It's in a restaurant in Chiba," says Ken.

"Don't forget! Ask the woman questions!" says Saho.

That day at work, Ken thinks about Saho and Yumiko's advice.

I have to learn many things, he thinks. *Next time, I will do a good job. I will not look at the menu for a long time. I will not talk about myself. I will ask the woman many questions. I will be a gentleman! Yumiko and Saho will be very surprised. And I will get a marriage partner!*

CHAPTER FOUR

Ken, his mother, his mother's friend, and her daughter are sitting in the hotel restaurant.

Ken remembers Yumiko's advice. *Ask the woman questions!*

So, he asks the woman many questions.

"Where do you work?"

"In an office," says the woman.

"Do you like your job?" asks Ken.

"Yes, I do."

"Why?" asks Ken.

"Why?" asks the woman. She is very surprised.

"Yes. Why do you like your job?" asks Ken.

"I like my job because I like my co-workers," says the woman.

"What time do you start and finish work?" asks Ken.

"I start at 8:30am and I usually finish at 5:30pm. Sometimes, I finish at 6:00pm."

"What are your hobbies?" asks Ken.

"My hobbies? Well…er…I like watching movies and listening to music," says the woman.

"What kind of music do you like?" asks Ken.

"I like J-POP," says the woman.

"Where do you listen to music?" asks Ken.

"Where? Where do I listen to music? Er…usually in my room, or in my car," says the woman.

"Do you like driving?" asks Ken.

"Yes, I do," says the woman.

"I like driving too. But I don't have a car," says Ken.

"Oh really?" asks the woman.

"No, but I have a bicycle," says Ken. "Do you have a bicycle?"

After the o-miai meeting, Ken and his mother go home. Ken is very happy. He asked many questions. But his mother is not happy.

"You asked too many questions Ken-chan!" says his mother.

"Too many?" asks Ken.

"Yes! Too many! It was like a job interview! The woman was very tired!" says his mother.

Later, Ken's mother's friend calls his mother. Her daughter does not want to see Ken again.

Ken is very disappointed. *Why not? I tried my best. I was polite. Yumiko and Saho said 'Ask questions!', so I asked many questions. What is the problem?*

Ken does not understand.

The next day, Ken goes to the office.

"How was your o-miai meeting?" asks Yumiko.

"It wasn't good. I failed," says Ken. "She doesn't want to see me again."

"Why not?" asks Yumiko.

"I asked too many questions. My mother was angry," says Ken.

"How many questions did you ask?" asks Saho.

"I don't know. But my mother said 'It was like a job interview!'" says Ken.

"Oh Ken! You need a balance! Only asking questions is not good!" says Saho.

"I know. But I get very nervous," says Ken.

"It's okay, Ken. Don't worry. We will help you! When is your next date?" asks Saho.

"I have a date with a woman from the Internet site next month," says Ken.

"Is it at a restaurant?" asks Yumiko.

"No, it isn't. It's at a coffee shop," says Ken.

"Okay, Saho and I will go, too!" says Yumiko. "We will watch you again!"

CHAPTER FIVE

Ken and the woman are in the coffee shop. They are drinking coffee and laughing. Yumiko and Saho are sitting at the next table. They are talking and watching Ken. Yumiko and Saho are very happy. Ken is doing a good job! His manners are very good.

When the waiter brought the menu, Ken asked the woman "What would you like?"

Also, he is communicating very well. He is asking some questions and the woman is asking some questions.

Ken and the woman finish eating. The waiter brings the bill.

Ken looks at the bill.

"Three thousand yen. So, that's one thousand five hundred yen each," says Ken.

The woman gives him one thousand five hundred yen. Ken looks at Saho and Yumiko. They are not smiling. They look angry again.

Why are they angry? What did I do wrong? he thinks.

On Monday morning, Saho and Yumiko talk to Ken.

"Did I pass?" asks Ken.

"Ken, on your date, you communicated very well. You asked questions and you talked about yourself a little. That's very good. Saho and I were very happy," says Yumiko.

"So why did you look angry?" asks Ken.

"Because you made a big mistake," says Saho.

Ken doesn't understand. "I made a mistake? What did I do?" he asks.

"The waiter brought the bill. You looked at it and then you said to the woman, 'That's one thousand five hundred yen each'," says Saho.

"Is that bad?" asks Ken.

"Yes it is!" says Yumiko. "The bill was only three thousand yen! You should say 'I will pay!'"

"Oh really? But, when I go drinking with you and Saho, we always split the bill," says Ken.

"Yes, we do. That is because we are friends. But a date is different!" says Saho.

"You should say, 'I will pay.' Then, some women might say 'No, we can split the bill 50-50.' Some women might say, 'Thank you very much.' But it is good manners to say 'I will pay'," says Yumiko. "It was only three thousand yen!"

Ken feels sad. He cannot do anything right. He always makes mistakes. "Maybe I will be a single man forever," he says.

"No, Ken. You will find a good wife. Don't worry," says Saho. "Yumiko and I are your Konkatsu Support Team! We will help you!"

"I have a good idea," says Yumiko. "How about a role-play?"

"A role-play? What's that?" asks Ken.

"Ken and Saho, you go to a café. Imagine it is a real date. Saho, imagine you meet Ken for the first time. Ken, imagine Saho is a woman from the Internet dating site. Saho, you check Ken's manners and actions. Then, you give feedback," says Yumiko.

"That's a good idea!" says Saho.

"Yes, it's a fantastic idea!" says Ken. "But, Saho, your boyfriend Kei will be very angry."

Saho looks upset. "Kei and I broke up," she says sadly.

"Oh really? That's too bad," says Ken.

"Yes, we broke up three months ago. His company transferred him to southern Japan. He lives in Kyushu now. It's very far from Tokyo, so we can't see each other. I was very sad. I cried very much. But now I'm OK. I want a boyfriend in Tokyo."

"So, you don't have a boyfriend?" asks Ken.

"No, I don't. I'm single," says Saho.

CHAPTER SIX

After work, Ken sits in the café. He waits for Saho. They will have a role-play date.

Saho walks into the café. Ken stands up.

"I'm Ken Maeda. Nice to meet you," says Ken.

"I'm Saho Mochida. Nice to meet you too," says Saho.

They sit down.

Ken shows Saho the menu. "What would you like to drink?" he says.

"I would like a cappuccino, please," says Saho.

"Would you like anything to eat?" asks Ken.

"Yes, I'll have some chocolate cake," says Saho.

The waiter comes to the table.

"A cappuccino and a café au lait, and two chocolate cakes, please," says Ken.

Saho and Ken talk. They imagine they are meeting for the first time. They talk about hobbies and family. They laugh a lot.

Then, Ken's phone rings. He answers it. It is his section manager.

"Hello. This is Ken Maeda speaking," he says. "Yes, Kacho…I understand…yes…of course…I will finish the report before Monday…yes…goodbye." Ken finishes the telephone call.

Five minutes later, Ken's phone rings again. Ken answers the phone.

"Hello. This is Ken Maeda speaking. Hello again Kacho…yes. I understand…yes…yes…goodbye."

Then, his phone rings again. And again. Every time, Ken answers

it. In total, his phone rings five times.
Saho is not happy.

CHAPTER SEVEN

It is Monday morning. Ken, Saho and Yumiko are talking in the office.

"How was the date?" asks Yumiko.

"It was good!" says Ken.

"It was not good," says Saho.

"What?!" says Ken. He is very shocked. "I showed you the menu. I asked you questions. I talked. We laughed. Then I paid!"

"Yes you did. But, you made a big mistake. You answered your phone," says Saho.

"But, Kacho called me! It was very important!" says Ken.

"But you answered your phone five times!" says Saho.

"Ken, on a date, answering the phone five times is not good," says Yumiko.

"But, Kacho called me! I had to answer my phone!" says Ken.

"Okay, I understand. But, did you say 'excuse me'? Or 'sorry'?" asks Yumiko.

"No, I didn't," says Ken. "Did I fail?"

"I'm sorry, Ken. You failed," says Saho.

Ken goes to the smoking room and lights a cigarette. He thinks Saho and Yumiko are too strict. He is trying his best, but they are never happy. Before, Ken, Saho and Yumiko had a good time at work. Now, they are always saying, 'Your manners are bad!' 'You made a mistake!' 'You failed!' Ken feels bad.

He thinks: *I have many friends. People say I am handsome. I am polite. I am kind. I have a good job with a good salary. I am good at my job. Why aren't*

15

Saho and Yumiko happy? Why don't women want to be my girlfriend? Saho and Yumiko have very high standards. Too high. I'm not perfect. I'm a normal human being. Why can't they understand? I think Saho and Yumiko are too strict.

He finishes his cigarette and goes back into the office.

"Don't worry Ken. Try again next week," says Yumiko. "Ken, take Saho to a restaurant."

"I don't know. I might give up on dating. Maybe I should stay single. Maybe I shouldn't get married, or look for a girlfriend," says Ken.

"No Ken! Don't give up! You are improving!" says Yumiko. "Take Saho to a restaurant! Try it one more time!"

"Ken, we want to help you! We are your friends!" says Saho.

Ken looks at Yumiko and Saho. They are smiling. They are strict, but they are very good friends and they are trying to help him.

"Okay, I will," says Ken. "One more time. One last chance."

For a week, Ken studies about dating manners on the internet. He writes the advice from Saho and Yumiko in a notebook.

This time, I will do a good job. My manners will be perfect! he thinks.

A week later, Saho and Ken go to a restaurant. This time, Ken's manners are very good. He shows Saho the menu. He selects his dish very quickly. He asks her questions and he talks about himself a little. He says "sorry" and "excuse me" when he answers a phone call from his manager. He offers to pay the bill. They have a very good time. Saho is very pleased. Ken is trying hard.

CHAPTER EIGHT

It is 8:00am on Monday morning. Saho and Yumiko are talking.

"How was Ken in the restaurant?" asks Yumiko.

"He was very good," says Saho. "He didn't ask too many questions. He offered to pay the bill. He was very charming."

"Great!" says Yumiko. "Did you have a good time, too?"

"Yes, I had a very good time," says Saho. "Ken doesn't need our help anymore."

"Really?" asks Yumiko.

"Yes, really," says Saho.

They smile, but Saho feels a little sad. She had a very good time with Ken. They laughed and talked a lot...

Ken comes into the office.

"Good morning!" says Ken.

"Good morning Ken!" say Saho and Yumiko.

Ken looks at Saho. "Thank you, Saho. I had a nice time on Saturday evening."

"Thank you Ken. I had a nice time, too."

"Congratulations Ken!" says Yumiko.

"Congratulations? Why? I don't understand," says Ken.

"You passed!" says Yumiko. "You don't need to go on role-play dates with Saho anymore!"

"Really?" asks Ken. He is very surprised. Then he feels a little sad. On Saturday night, he had a good time with Saho. He wants to go on another date with her. He wants to spend time with her.

"You look sad Ken. Why? This is happy news. Your manners are very good now. You can find a girlfriend easily," says Yumiko.

"Oh, I'm not sad. Of course not. I'm happy," says Ken. "Thank you. Thank you very much."

But Ken wants to go on a date with Saho. What can he do? He thinks for a few seconds. Then, he has an idea.

"Saho, I am still nervous about dating. My manners are not perfect yet. Could we go on a date one more time?" asks Ken. "I need to check my second date manners."

Saho and Yumiko are surprised.

"Yes, of course," says Saho. She smiles at Ken. She had a good time with Ken. She wants to spend more time with him.

CHAPTER NINE

It is Saturday night. Ken and Saho are in a restaurant. They are eating and drinking. They are having a very good time.

They talk about many things. They talk about work, and their lives.

Ken's manners are very good.

Then, he stops talking.

"Are you okay Ken?" asks Saho. "You are very quiet."

"Yes, I am fine. But, I want to tell you something."

"Okay, go ahead," says Saho.

"I like you," says Ken.

"Pardon?" Saho is very surprised.

"I like you," says Ken.

"Ken, 'I like you' is very direct. It is only the second date. The woman will be very shocked," says Saho. When you see women from the Internet dating site, don't say 'I like you' on the second date".

"No, Saho, you don't understand. I like you," says Ken.

Saho looks at Ken. She doesn't understand.

"Is this still a role-play date?" asks Saho. "Is this still a practice date?"

"No, this is not a role-play. This is not practice. This is not imagination. I like YOU Saho," says Ken. "YOU, Saho Mochida, my co-worker."

Saho is very surprised. She looks at Ken. He is a very kind man. He is a hard worker and he is very friendly. When they go out, they have a very good time.

Saho smiles. She feels shy.

"I like you too Ken," she says quietly.

"Really? Really?" asks Ken. "Really? You like me?"

"Yes, really. You are a very nice man. And you try your best to improve your manners," says Saho. "You are a very hard worker."

"Saho, are you looking for a new boyfriend?" asks Ken.

"Yes, I am. I was very sad when my boyfriend went to Kyushu and we split up. But now I'm fine. I want to find a boyfriend soon. I want a boyfriend in Tokyo," says Saho.

"Saho, can I be your boyfriend?" asks Ken.

Saho is very surprised. "Pardon?"

"I said, 'Can I be your boyfriend?'" says Ken. He feels very nervous.

"Oh, yes, of course! Thank you Ken! I am happy to be your girlfriend!" says Saho.

Ken and Saho order champagne. They celebrate. They are both very surprised.

They didn't expect to become a couple.

"Yumiko will be very surprised!" says Ken.

"Yes, she will! I'll tell her on Monday!" says Saho.

Ken and Saho smile at each other. They are a very cute couple!

CHAPTER TEN

It is Monday morning. Saho tells Yumiko the news.

"Yumiko I have some good news! Ken and I are a couple!" says Saho.

"Really? Oh great! Great! Wonderful! My plan worked!" says Yumiko.

Saho looks at Yumiko.

"Pardon? Your plan? What plan?" asks Saho.

"My plan! It was my plan from the start!" says Yumiko.

"What? I don't understand," says Saho.

"Ken wanted a girlfriend. You wanted a boyfriend. I had a good idea. My idea was: You go on a role-play date with Ken, and fall in love! Great! Perfect! It was my plan!"

"You planned this?!" asks Saho.

"Yes, I did," says Yumiko. "Are you pleased? Or are you angry?"

"I'm pleased of course!" says Saho. "And very surprised!"

They both laugh.

Ken comes into the office.

"Congratulations, Ken!" says Yumiko.

"Oh, did Saho tell you?" asks Ken. "We are a couple!"

"Ken, it was Yumiko's plan! She arranged it!" says Saho.

"What? Yumiko's plan? Really?" Ken is very surprised. He looks at Yumiko. "Thank you Yumiko. I am very happy. Thanks to you, Saho and I are a couple."

Then, the department manager, Fuji bucho, comes into the office.

"Maeda san! Please come into my office!" says Fuji bucho.

"Yes, Fuji bucho," says Ken.

He goes into Fuji bucho's office.

Saho and Yumiko talk.

"Do you want to marry Ken?" asks Yumiko.

"Yes, I think so!" says Saho. "He is a very nice man. Ken and I have been friends and co-workers for many years. I know he is a kind man. And, he is very handsome!"

"Yes, he is," says Yumiko. "You are lucky Saho! You have a handsome and kind boyfriend! And he has very good manners too!"

Five minutes later, Ken comes out of Fuji bucho's office. He looks very sad. He sits down at his desk.

"Ken, are you okay?" asks Yumiko.

Ken looks at the floor. "No, I am not okay," he says.

"What's wrong?" asks Saho.

"I have some bad news," says Ken.

"Bad news? What?" asks Saho. She is very worried.

"Fuji bucho gave me some very, very bad news," says Ken.

"What is it? Tell us!" says Yumiko.

"Next month, I have to transfer to another office," says Ken.

"Transfer? Where to?" asks Saho.

"To Yonago City," says Ken.

"Yonago City?" say Saho and Yumiko.

"Where is Yonago City?" asks Saho.

"It's in Tottori Prefecture, in west Japan," says Ken.

"Tottori Prefecture?!" says Saho. "That's really far from Tokyo!"

"Ken, Saho, what are you going to do?" asks Yumiko.

Ken and Saho look at each other. Saho doesn't want another long-distance relationship. She wants a boyfriend in Tokyo. She doesn't know what to do.

What will happen to Ken and Saho?

Find out in Ken's Story Part 2, also available from I Talk You Talk Press.

22

THANK YOU

Thank you for reading Ken's Story Part 1. (Word count: 4,614) We hope you enjoyed it.

There are quizzes about this book on our free study site I Talk You Talk Press EXTRA. http://italk-youtalk.com

If you would like to read more graded readers, please visit our website http://www.italkyoutalk.com

Other Level 1 graded readers include
A Business Trip to New York
A Homestay in Auckland
A Trip to London
Dear Ellen
Haruna's Story Part 1
Haruna's Story Part 2
Haruna's Story Part 3
Ken's Story Part 2
Life is Surprising!
Strange Stories
The Christmas Present
The Old Hospital
We Met Online

ABOUT THE AUTHOR

I Talk You Talk Press is a Japan-based publisher of language textbooks, graded readers and language learning/teaching resources.

Our team is made up of highly experienced language teachers and translators, who have all studied at least one additional language to an advanced level.

This experience enables us to design our materials from the perspective of both the teacher and the learner. We consult with both teachers and language learners when designing our textbooks and graded readers, and test our materials extensively in the classroom before publication.

We are a fast-growing press, and currently publish graded readers for learners of English. We publish new graded readers monthly.

www.ingramcontent.com/pod-product-compliance
Lightning Source LLC
Chambersburg PA
CBHW022352040426
42449CB00006B/836